of Appleby.

GEOGRAPHIA

Picturesque
LAKELAND
ONE HUNDRED
YEARS AGO

Compiled by Frank Graham
From Old Prints

Jacket designed by Frank Varty

FRANK GRAHAM
6 Queen's Terrace, Newcastle upon Tyne, 2.

Published 1969

© 900409 62 2

Printed in Great Britain by Fletcher & Son Ltd, Norwich
Bound by Richard Clay (The Chaucer Press) Ltd, Bungay, Suffolk

FOREWORD

In the following pages we present a picture of Lakeland in the first half of the nineteenth century. We have used one hundred and fifty old prints to show what the towns and villages of Cumberland, Westmorland and northern Lancashire were like in those days. The lake and mountain scenery, the roads, the inns and taverns are illustrated as they were before the coming of the motor car. The area covered stretches from Kendal to Carlisle covering most of the three Lakeland counties.

A little over half the prints are by Thomas Allom and are taken from his well-known book—*Westmorland, Cumberland, Durham and Northumberland* —published in 1832. This work was the most popular illustrated book of the northern counties ever published and thousands of copies were sold. It was a magnificent production. The lithographic views of Carlisle are from M. E. Nutter's book, *Carlisle in the Olden Time*, 1832. The fine large views of the Keswick area by William Westall are taken from his rare work, *Views of the Lake and Vale of Keswick*, published in 1820. Some smaller views are by the same artist and are from *Great Britain Illustrated*, 1830.

There are several small vignettes which were published about the middle of the nineteenth century. They are by W. Banks, an Edinburgh artist and publisher, who issued many small books containing this type of view. The local agent for these publications was J. Garnet of Windermere under whose imprint they appeared. The larger vignettes are from various books by J. Harwood, particularly his *Scenery of Great Britain* published in the eighteen forties.

The remaining views are from a variety of sources. Most of the prints are reproduced in the same size as the originals, but a few have been reduced.

It will be noticed that some of the dates in the List of Plates do not coincide with the publication of the book from which they are taken. This is due to the fact that the prints were sometimes engraved a year or two earlier. Where the date is given on the print this is the one we have used.

STRAMMONGATE BRIDGE, KENDAL.

KENDAL, FROM GREEN BANK.

KENDAL, FROM THE CASTLE.

KENDAL, WESTMORLAND.

SCOUT SCAR, NEAR KENDAL, WESTMORLAND.

LEVINS HALL, WESTMORLAND.

Drawn by G. Pickering.

Engraved by R. Roberts.

NEWBY BRIDGE, LANCASHIRE.

FURNESS ABBEY HOTEL,
VALE OF NIGHTSHADE.
THOS SLAVEY, PROPRIETOR.

WINDERMERE
from near Storrs.

NEWBY BRIDGE

Waterhead from the Queen Hotel.

THE FERRY, WINDERMERE.

WRAY CASTLE, WINDERMERE.

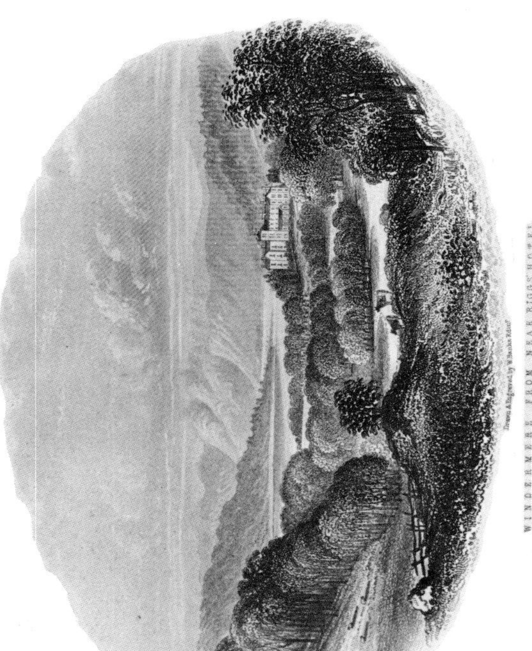

WINDERMERE, FROM NEAR RIGG'S HOTEL.

HEAD OF WINDERMERE LAKE.

THE LOW WOOD HOTEL.

FROM THE LANDING PLACE AT WRAY CASTLE,

WINDERMERE.

STORRS, WINDERMERE LAKE.

The Ferry Point, Windermere Lake, Westmoreland.

15

Bowneſs

The Village of Bonness

Windermere

Storrs Point, Windermere, Westmoreland.

Windermere from Bowness.

Winandermere Lake from Calgarth.

WINDERMERE LAKE, FROM LOW WOOD INN.

Drawn by G. Pickering.

Engraved by V. Le Petit.

WINDERMERE LAKE, LOOKING DOWN.

FERRY HOUSE REGATTA; WINDERMERE LAKE.

BOWNESS, & WINDERMERE LAKE, WESTMORLAND.

WINDERMERE LAKE, FROM THE FERRY HOUSE.

STORRS HALL, WINDERMERE LAKE, WESTMORLAND.

LOW-WOOD HOTEL

WINDERMERE

VALLEY OF TROUTBECK, WESTMORLAND.

VIEW NEAR AMBLESIDE

Ambleside, Westmorland.

AMBLESIDE, WESTMORLAND.

THE MILL, ON THE STOCK-GILL, NEAR AMBLESIDE.

BRIDGE HOUSE, AMBLESIDE, WESTMORLAND.

25

DUNGEON GILL, WESTMORLAND.

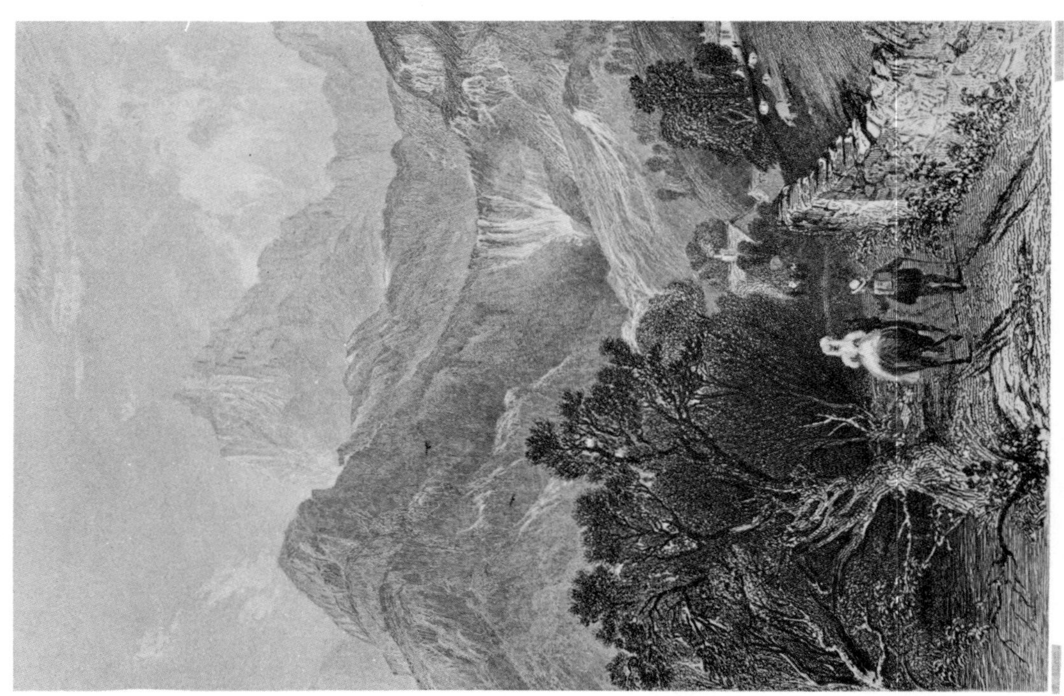

MILL BECK, GREAT LANGDALE.

26

SCAWFELL PIKES, FROM STY HEAD, CUMBERLAND.

THRANG CRAG SLATE QUARRY, GREAT LANGDALE, WESTMORLAND.

(THE PROPERTY OF LORD LOWTHER.)

SKELWITH BRIDGE, WESTMORLAND.

HAWKSHEAD HALL.

STICKLE TARN, LANGDALE PIKES, FROM PAVEY ARK, WESTMORLAND.

Conistone Water

Lancashire

THE WATERHEAD INN,   CONISTON.

THE PROPERTY OF J.G.MARSHALL, ESQ M.P.

ESTHWAITE WATER.
From the Ulverston Road.

RYDAL WATER.

CONISTON
from the wood above Bank ground

RYDAL WATER FROM UNDER LOUGHRIGG FELL.

Rydal Lake, Westmoreland

RYDAL HALL FROM FOX HOW, WESTMORLAND.

VALE OF GRASMERE, CUMBERLAND.

GRASMERE from RED BANK.

Grasmere.

GRASSMERE LAKE & VILLAGE, WESTMORLAND.

GRASSMERE FROM BUTTER CRAGS, WESTMORLAND.

GRASSMERE FROM LOUGHRIGG FELL.

ELTERWATER. GREAT LANGDALE. WESTMORLAND.

Dunmail Raise Cumberland.

CASTLE ROCK, VALE OF ST JOHN, LOOKING SOUTH, CUMBERLAND.

Saddleback from the Vale of St John.

WATENLATH, & THE STREAM OF LOWDORE.

THIRLMERE BRIDGE, LOOKING NORTH, CUMBERLAND.

THIRLMERE, OR WYTHBURN WATER, CUMBERLAND.

THIRLMERE & HELVELLEN &c, FROM RAVEN CRAG.

VALE OF KESWICK.

DERWENTWATER.

THIRLMERE FROM RAVEN CRAG.

Lodore Cumberland.

DERWENT WATER, & LOWDORE, CUMBERLAND.

DERWENTWATER, & VILLAGE OF GRANGE, FROM THE ENTRANCE TO BORROWDALE.

DERWENT-WATER, FROM APPLETHWAITE.

DERWENT WATER, FROM THE CASTLE HEAD, CUMBERLAND.

Derwentwater & Keswick from Skiddaw.

G. Pickering   A. Le Petit

DERWENT & BASSENTHWAITE LAKES,—KESWICK & SKIDDAW IN THE DISTANCE, CUMBERLAND.

KESWICK, FROM GRETA BRIDGE.

GRETA HALL AND KESWICK BRIDGE.

THE DRUIDS' STONES, NEAR KESWICK.

Skiddaw & Bassenthwaite Water.

Skiddaw.

Drawn & Engraved by W. Westall, A.R.A.

BASSENTHWAITE LAKE LOOKING SOUTH, CUMBERLAND.

COCKERMOUTH.

Drawn & Engraved by W. Westall, A.R.A.

Portinscale Bridge

near Keswick.

BLEY-WATER TARN FROM THE TOP OF THE HIGH STREET MOUNTAIN.

SMALL-WATER TARN: FROM NANBIELD, LOOKING INTO MARDALE.

ELEA TARN, WESTMORLAND.

STY HEAD TARN, CUMBERLAND.

ROSSTHWAITE, BORROWDALE, FROM THE ROAD TO WATENLATH.

KESWICK, DERWENT, &c. FROM THE ROAD TO KENDAL.

BORROWDALE, CUMBERLAND.

CASTLE CRAG, BORROWDALE, FROM THE VILLAGE OF GRANGE, CUMBERLAND.

Borrowdale from Stye Head.

Bowder Stone. Borrowdale.

EAGLE CRAG FROM ROSTHWAITE, BORROWDALE.

Crummock Water & Buttermere.

Inn at Buttermere.

The Birth Place of Mary Robinson.

Buttermere Hawze.

57

BUTTERMERE. CUMBERLAND.

BUTTERMERE LAKE & VILLAGE. CUMBERLAND.

LOWESWATER, FROM WATER END, CUMBERLAND.

CRUMMOCK WATER, CUMBERLAND.

CRUMMOCK & BUTTERMERE LAKES

BORROWDALE
near the Bowder Stone

BASSENTHWAITE LAKE

ENNERDALE

FURNESS ABBEY SOUTH EAST.

WASDALE HALL—WAST WATER.

HONISTER CRAG
from the Quarry Road to Yew Crag.

WASTWATER

WASTWATER, CUMBERLAND.

Wast Water Cumberland.

WHITEHAVEN, CUMBERLAND.

ENNERDALE WATER, FROM HOW HALL, CUMBERLAND.

Ullswater.

FROM THE MATTERDALE ROAD.

From a painting in the possession of H. Howard. Esq.ʳ Greystoke Castle.

GOLDRILL BECK & ULLSWATER, CUMBERLAND.

ULLSWATER FROM POOLY BRIDGE.

Ullswater near Patterdale.

Ulleswater, Cumberland.

PATTERDALE BRIDGE, WESTMORLAND.

VIEW OF ULLESWATER, LOOKING TOWARDS PATTERDALE.

PATTERDALE, GOING TOWARDS AMBLESIDE, WESTMORLAND.

SECOND REACH, OF ULSWATER.

UPPER REACH, ULLSWATER.

BROTHER'S WATER FROM KIRKSTONE FOOT, WESTMORELAND.

UPPER REACH OF ULLSWATER.

ULLSWATER.

LEATHE'S WATER.

BROTHER'S WATER.

GRISDALE, NEAR ULLESWATER, WESTMORLAND.

HAWES-WATER, FROM THWAITE-FORCE, WESTMORLAND.

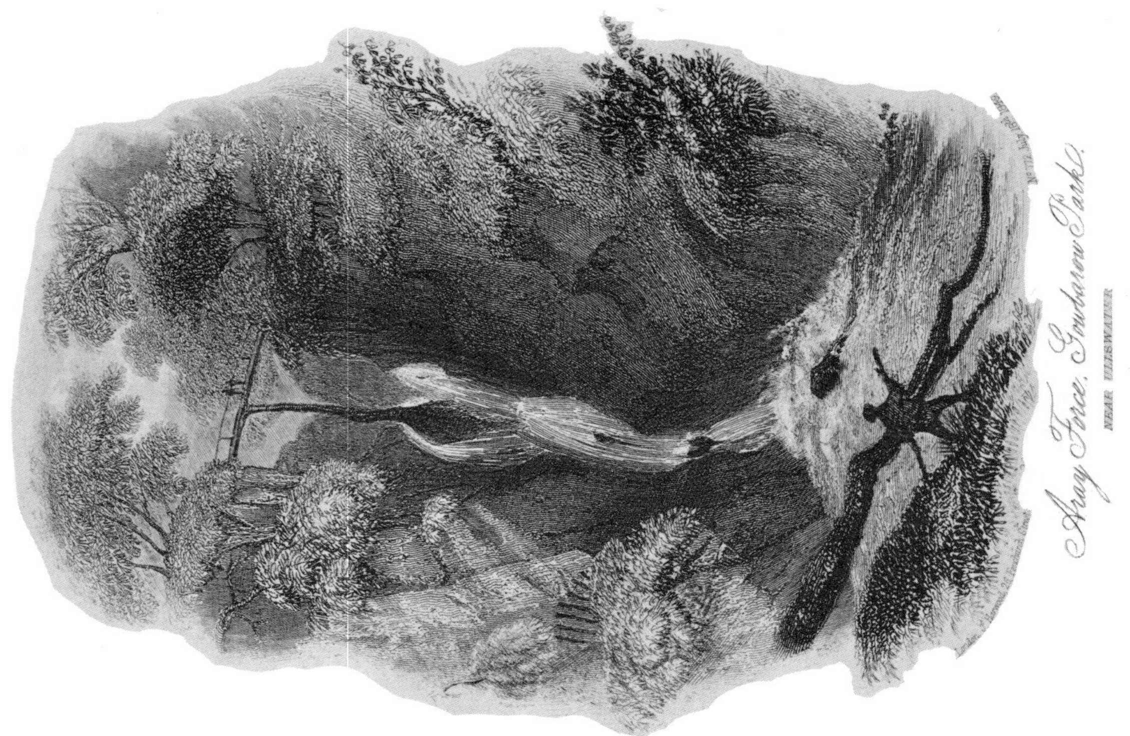

Aray Force, Gowbarrow Park.

NEAR ULLSWATER.

AIREY FORCE, CUMBERLAND.

SOUTH VIEW OF LOWTHER CASTLE.

LOWTHER CASTLE & PARK, WESTMORLAND.

BROUGHAM CASTLE, WESTMORLAND.

EAMONT BRIDGE, FROM THE WESTMORLAND SIDE.

THE GIANT'S GRAVE, IN THE CHURCH YARD, PENRITH.

Penrith Castle, Cumberland.

Drawn by T. Hearne
Engraved by Will.m Byrne

To his Grace Cha.s Howard Duke of Norfolk, hereditary Earl Marshal of England
This VIEW of GREYSTOKE CASTLE
Is inscribed by his Grace's most obedient Servants Thomas Hearne and William Byrne

SOLA VIRTUS INVICTA

London. Publish'd as the Act directs 1 Jan. 1778, by W. Byrne, Welbe Street, Oxford Str. & T. Hearne, at M.r Garvock's, corner of S.t Martins Street, Leicester Square.

To the Reverend The Dean and Chapter of Carlisle.
This View of **WETHERELL PRIORY** is inscribed,
By their most obedient Servants, Thomas Hearne and William Byrne.

London. Publish'd as the Act directs 15 April 1779. by W.ᵐ Byrne & Tho.ˢ Hearne.

Carlisle Castle.

Sparrow sculp.

T. Allom.

J. Sands.

CARLISLE CATHEDRAL, CUMBERLAND.

Drawn by M E Nutter from an Original Sketch.

On Zinc by A Picken.

THE TOWN HALL of CARLISLE in 1780.

Drawn by M E Nutter from the original sketch

Giles lithout

CARLISLE FROM NEAR STANWIX BANK

UPWARDS OF ONE HUNDRED YEARS AGO

The Arms of